COLUMBIA COLLEGE CHICAGO

3 2711 00093 1265

D1537466

ENTERED JAN 1 0 2006

COLUMBIA COLLEGE LIBRARY
600 S. MICHIGAN AVENUE
CHICAGO, IL 60605

Just My Imagination

Acknowledgements

Curated by
Kim Moodie   David Merritt

Organized by the MMB Collective and Museum London

This publication was produced with additional support
from the following:

Art Gallery of Windsor
Phyllis and Alan Cohen
Dalhousie Art Gallery
Illingworth Kerr Gallery
Mendel Art Gallery
Michael Gibson Gallery
Museum of Contemporary Canadian Art
Nicholas Metivier Gallery Inc.
Orthoconcept Qué. Inc.
Paul Petro Contemporary Art
Pierre-François Ouellette Art Contemporain Inc.
Robert Birch Gallery
Trépanier Baer Gallery Inc.

Itinerary

Museum London
November 6, 2004 - February 27, 2005
and
ArtLab, John Labatt Visual Arts Centre, University of Western Ontario
November 12, 2004 - January 23, 2005

Art Gallery of Windsor
April 16 – June 12, 2005

Museum of Canadian Contemporary Art
July 16 – August 21, 2005

Dalhousie Art Gallery
October 13 – November 27, 2005

Mendel Art Gallery
January 27 – March 5, 2006

Art Gallery of Algoma
May 25 – August 7, 2006

Illingworth Kerr Gallery
October 19 – November 18, 2006

Southern Alberta Art Gallery
January 20 – March 4, 2007

Contents

8   Foreword MMB

9   Foreword Museum London

11   *Drawing as...*
David Merritt   Kim Moodie

21   *Just My Imagination?*
Kym Pruesse

26   Stephen Andrews

28   Sheila Butler

31   *Recording the World – Drawing Today*
Daina Augaitis

32   Lucie Chan

34   Cathy Daley

37   *Moving on Drawing*
Cliff Eyland

38   Raphaëlle de Groot

40   Michelle Gay

43   *The Moving Finger*
Robin Metcalfe

44   Luanne Martineau

46   Jason McLean

49   *Contemporary Drawing Practices*
David Liss

50   Alison Norlen

52   Ed Pien

55   *A Brief Treatise on the Line*
Louise Déry

56   John Scott

58   Candice Tarnowski

61   *A little History for a Lot of Drawing: A View from Halifax*
Susan Gibson Garvey

64   David Tomas

66   Anna Torma

68   Works in the Exhibition

69   Biographies - Artists in the Exhibition

71   Biographies - Catalogue Contributors

72   Credits

Foreword

[MMB Collective]

The MMB Collective is Kim Moodie, David Merritt and Sheila Butler. It was formed in 2002 around the vision of an exhibition, national in scope, of recent drawing-based works by contemporary Canadian artists. Founded on an enthusiasm that grows out of a personal investment in drawing as a key component of our own work, this project celebrates the power of drawing — particularly its ability to describe material and psychic reality. Through the efficacy of the imagination, drawing propels the creation of a world around us.

The division of tasks among the three members of this collective evolved organically, with Kim Moodie and David Merritt assuming curatorial responsibilities and Sheila Butler participating as an exhibiting artist and project coordinator. A series of two cross-country studio tours provided the basis for the selection of artists and works for the exhibition. Guiding this selection was an emphasis on representational imagery stemming from each artist's imagination, with symbols evolving from the lived reality of drawing processes. Leading up to the exhibition opening, two visiting artists' residencies were organized in London to provide living testimony to immediacy of drawing in processes of artistic production. Conjointly with the opening of *Just My Imagination*, we also organized a national symposium to stimulate critical dialogue around the dynamics of current drawing-based practices.

What needs and aesthetic virtues are driving the expanding field of contemporary drawing? We propose the *Just My Imagination* exhibition, related residencies and symposium as ways to examine and enjoy this gratifying phenomenon in current Canadian art.

This project, in its early development, would not have been possible without the passionate support of Patrick Mahon, Chair of the Department of Visual Arts at the University of Western Ontario and the moral and financial support of Phyllis and Alan Cohen. Brian Meehan, Executive Director of Museum London was also invaluable, expressing his personal enthusiasm for the project in the early stages and generously offering the exhibition a second venue. Happily, the project was met with similar support nationally when we proposed the exhibition for tour to the Art Gallery of Algoma, Art Gallery of Windsor, Dalhousie Art Gallery, Illingworth Kerr Gallery, Mendel Art Gallery, the Museum of Contemporary Canadian Art, and the Southern Alberta Art Gallery, making possible a cross-country tour for this national exhibition. We thank Museum London for generously providing critical logistical support. But at the head of this long line, our gratitude to the fourteen artists who comprise *Just My Imagination*. Their commitment to providing, and in many cases, creating, major work has made this project an enriching and inspiring experience for us all.

David Merritt   Kim Moodie   Sheila Butler
MMB Collective

Foreword

Just My Imagination is an exhibition that is ambitious in scope, provocative in content, and investigates the current state of drawing-based art practice in Canada. It provides an opportunity to see the diversity of work being made today and challenges us to expand our idea of drawing well beyond the traditional notion of marks on paper.

The MMB Collective (Sheila Butler, David Merritt, Kim Moodie) are to be congratulated, not only for conceiving of the project, but for their dedication and endurance in maintaining their enthusiasm as *Just My Imagination* grew to, what I can only assume, were unimagined heights. The depth of research that went into the selection of artists and works, as well as the development of a national tour for the exhibition, are accomplishments for which they can be justifiably proud.

The exhibition and subsequent tour would not be possible without the support of the artists and lenders, John Latour, Wesley Yuen and Patrick Prinster, Julia and Gilles Ouellette, and Orthoconcept Qué. Inc., who have made work available.

We have a long-standing history of partnerships with the Visual Arts Department of the University of Western Ontario and we are once again proud to collaborate by being co-presenters of *Just My Imagination* in London. My thanks to Patrick Mahon and all those involved with the Art Lab at UWO for their cooperation on this project.

I would like to acknowledge Melanie Townsend, Museum London's Curator of Contemporary Art, who joined Museum London in the midst of the planning of this exhibition and tour, for jumping into the deep end and ably guiding all aspects of the project this past year. Thanks to donors Phyllis and Alan Cohen whose early financial contribution facilitated the development of this project in it's initial stages. Thanks also go to Kim Clarke for his photography of the installations; Bob Ballantine for his design of this publication; writers, Daina Augaitis, Louise Déry, Cliff Eyland, Susan Gibson Garvey, David Liss, Robin Metcalfe, Kym Preusse, for their contributions to the publication; and to Jim Drobnick for his time and skill in editing the texts.

This publication has been made possible through the financial support of a large number of people and organizations. We are extremely grateful to them. In addition to the support provided by many of the touring venues, financial support for this publication was also provided by Robert Birch Gallery, Michael Gibson Gallery, Nicholas Metivier Gallery, Orthoconcept Qué. Inc., Pierre-François Ouellette Art Contemporain, Paul Petro Contemporary Art, and Trépanier Baer Gallery.

Finally, the support of the Canada Council for the Arts through their Programming and Operations Assistance Program, the Ontario Arts Council, and the City of London allow us to bring this type of exhibition programming before our publics. Their ongoing support is very much appreciated.

Brian Meehan
Director, Museum London

Anna Torma, *Draw me a monster: Bestiary III,* 2004 (detail) Photo: David Merritt

Drawing as ...

[David Merritt   Kim Moodie]

... a barrier of braided links that leaks like a wicker basket but can still function as a dam.

Michel Serres[1]

JOHN BERGER ONCE PROPOSED that drawing could be categorized in three ways: as studies of the visible world, as re-envisioned memories, or as constructs from the imagination. Closely considered, the three appear interconnected. In order to depict memories and the imagination, Berger suggested that artists commonly rely on the conventions of representational drawing. Conversely, he described drawings of the visible world as "interrogating the strangeness, the enigma, of what is before our eyes."[2] Across these categories, figurative drawing can be seen as tracing a shifting threshold between the seen and the unseen — the previously known and the yet known. It crosses acculturated experience with desire, fear or profound equivocation.

The drawing-based works in *Just My Imagination* envision a world where psychic, social and material processes are intimately entwined. These are works given to exploring unstable conditions of transition and transformation. They may, in the course of their development, stray from more orthodox approaches to drawing. In terms of both materiality and imagery, the drawings featured in *Just My Imagination* appear alternately familiar and estranged, direct and mediated, seductive and grotesque. In the mutable manner of the imaginary, these works can seem simultaneously one *and* the other.

Across the range of artists' practices in *Just My Imagination*, drawing can be seen offering an accessible means of binding the comprehensible and the incomprehensible through sight, mind and touch. It also offers an immediate way of engaging and reconstituting the disjunctive information and events that have become the pulse of daily life. Whether using familiar materials and techniques, or translating these into media customarily seen as contrary to its traditions, the activity of drawing in *Just My Imagination* comprises an illuminated root system — one capable of issuing and sustaining the most diverse varieties of visual practice.

To Begin: Drawing Is...

The words "Drawing is..." begin a sentence that is difficult to complete. Whether approached as a general set of material conditions (such as "unique works on paper"), or techniques (such as line or mark-making), or functions (such as preparatory or investigative tactics), the practice of drawing seems resistant, or indifferent, to reductive definitions. As a discipline, its processes are typically additive and open; they are as receptive to revision and reversal as they are to progressive refinement. Born of expedience and indulgent of impulse, drawing's materials are traditionally handy, flexible and expendable. On a technical level, its work can be achieved with any tool that can render a mark, from a line traced in sand, through fine art media such as charcoal on paper, to the virtual vocabularies of digital rendering and display. Among its approaches, drawing can include both unschooled and highly refined mark-making, loose-limbed mind's eye impressions and carefully scrutinized studies from life. And though its practices have resulted in a wealth of completely self-sustaining works, the languages of drawing remain potentially transferable to practically any other visual discipline. In itself, it seems, drawing is still perfectly equipped to venture out from itself. In this light, Paul Klee's adage, "Formation is good. Form is bad"[3] could be invoked to describe the mobile and multiform language of drawing just as it can describe the increasingly migratory practices of contemporary artists who have come to exploit its resources.

Contingency and Autonomy

Viewed within a hierarchy of visual disciplines evolving since Vasari's time, drawing has appeared a somewhat misplaced object. Located between such media specializations as painting, sculpture and architecture, it has functioned ambiguously at both the foundation

John Scott has inscribed a muscle car with the Book of Revelations, and drawn benign skull bunny people shadowed by airborne death machines, strong commentary on macho nihilism. Substitute for the Prayer Wheel *includes fifteen drawings arranged in a loose grid, mounted on top of a wall of printed scrolls. The lines of black ink text endlessly repeat the same Tibetan prayer for peace. The innumerable lines, their characters moving slightly up and down, suggest an electrified, humming field of energy, a chant. The fifteen drawings are referential metaphors for a multitude of issues: deforestation, disarmament, stem cell research, space exploration, transgender ambiguity and so on. Scott's drawing techniques are direct, his feelings expressively visible. Much of his work is grounded in an angst that is relative to awareness today — so many concerns, so little done. In one drawing, a bunny person waits in a cocoon, preparing to start over. Overall, Scott produced the piece in affiliation with a group called Team Apocalypse. The work suggests that change will occur only through a manifestation of spiritual values realized by repeated collective energies.*

*The image of an actress — her upper body a photograph, her lower body an ink drawing — dangles in front of a hand-held paper on a computer screen. She systematically brushes a changing time and date stamp off her arm. Initially, her gesture seems natural, but with repetition, it appears rehearsed. On another computer, viewers manipulate a mouse to swing and bounce a figure across the background of a film still of a studio. In panoramic scenes, ink-drawn boats and small beings prance across cropped photo landscapes of dirt, sand and snow. Using mathematical algorithms, **Michelle Gay** creates codes that can place and animate drawings in digital space. And these spaces are particular. The paper is a white backdrop. The studio is an assembled scene for conceiving and performing. Long panoramas imply narratives. The framed areas of dust, sand and snow are removed minimal planes, defined only by light, shadows and receding textured materiality. Gay seems to acknowledge that digital space is a progression in Modernism's embrace of technology. Computers are another ground for using determined forms, processed means and staged settings. Yet her unique development of codes and the placement of her fluid surreal figures in mechanized space suggest a rupture, a need to insert the personal and poetic into the ordained.*

and margins of artists' practices in the West. Although prized by collectors for its intimacy and immediacy since the sixteenth century, drawing's value as an autonomous medium has been long linked to its relative contingency as a practice. Whether thumbnail sketch or carefully crafted "presentation drawing,"[4] its customary place has been one set literally before, or beneath, disciplines seen possessing greater visual resolve — and broader cultural significance. Associated with preparatory processes traditionally considered of greater worth to the studio or classroom than the larger public, drawing has tended to play a relatively minor role in art historical and critical discourses. Rarely, if ever, has its production alone been considered a sufficient basis for an ambitious artistic practice. Through the latter part of the twentieth century however, this perspective appears to have shifted. The increased centrality of drawing within artists' practices, as well as its prominence in international exhibitions, has brought repeated claims for recognition of its value as an equal and independent discipline. Though it may be interesting to speculate on the relationship between drawing's rising fortunes and the many critical challenges put to Modernist notions of aesthetic autonomy at the end of the last century, it remains clear that the relative contingency of drawing has not diminished with its growing independent stature. Despite lively and ongoing revisions in premise and purpose, diversifying technical means, and increases in the scale and scope of its projects, recent drawing appears as rigorously committed to the open-ended and transitive as it does to the primary value of its outcomes.

Drawing in the Vernacular

Apart from art histories and collections, drawing actually slipped out from under the decorum of greater works and into public view well before its recent resurgence. The traditional meaning of *cartoon*, as a

*There is no one present in **Alison Norlen**'s charcoal perspectives of carnival grounds and desolate industrialized disaster sites. These illusionistic panoramas amplify excess and entertainment, and are energized by an immense display of artistic versatility. Yet the lack of living creatures suggests that viewers, as visitors, are nomads enthralled with spectacle wanderlust. The use of strong colour is a recent development in her work. In Untitled, an electric blue both intensifies and cools the scene. At twenty feet long, the expansive drawing overwhelms the peripheral capacity for vision. A sight line divides the artwork: a modern, open pit mine occupies the lower half, which is then backed by immense Ferris wheels and the vastness of forest and mountains. Visible textures stir upon the surface, but conveyor belts sit still, roads are empty, and block houses deserted. Loneliness pervades the scene. The abandoned mine seems purposeless, symbolizing the wasting of nature's resources.*

*On a model's platform, dressed in coveralls, **Raphaëlle de Groot** staples large sheets of paper together, and then wraps them about her head, each layer fixed with masking tape. Next she uses a long-handled paintbrush to mark features on the white mass. Eventually she slits the cocoon and slides it off. Her performance is videotaped and university art students draw the progressive stages of her appearance. Possible interpretations emerge — she is a butterfly, a science fiction insect, a monster, a subjectively-oriented modern artist. A variety of emotional and psychological states also surface: fragility, foresight, monotony, self-absorption — the markings of the unconscious on a white ground. Previously de Groot has asked blind individuals to draw objects traced by their hands, and collected dust from an abandoned factory floor and glued it, Braille-like, onto scrolls. In an Italian textile factory she solicited written expressions by placing letterboxes in the various departments. Her exhibitions and catalogues document these activities. Here she shows four monitors arranged on a platform, allowing her videotaped performance to be viewed from all directions. Displayed on nearby walls are over one hundred and twenty student drawings. More are archived as books on nearby tables. She resists the role of the narcissistic loner and contests the hierarchies traditionally inherent between artist, artwork, subject and model. Instead, de Groot nurtures communal exchange, providing conduits that help externalize the experiences of others. The immediacy and tactility of writing, drawing or reading Braille, facilitates participation and involvement.*

drawn-to-scale transfer drawing (described by Robin Metcalfe elsewhere in this publication), now appears all but lost to present-day understanding. While still lending itself to the purposes of transfer, the modern-era cartoon is not subsumed into a more fulsome or sophisticated visual form — rather, even in translation to print, its image remains fundamentally unaltered. This drawing, delivered unembellished into the plain light of day, is brought to inhabit a less socially privileged and refined world. Adapted to the conflicted spaces of daily life, the cartoon has become a drawing genre full of ladders with broken rungs, leading up and down, and nowhere. It is interesting that recent drawing practice, in similarly slipping out on its own into the wider world, has come to revisit the cartoon and other vernacular genres once seen as the antithesis of the canonical concerns of drawing. In *Just My Imagination*, the more classical figurative idioms of gestural mark-making and modeled drawing can be seen taking up common space with the stylistic conventions of cartoons and comics — as well as those found in scientific diagrams, book illustration and animation. Similarly, following this vernacular turn, hand-rendered translations of photography, mechanical printing, and digital media resurface here — alongside those works that translate the hand-rendered into mechanically or electronically mediated forms.

Drawing as....

Hubert Damisch once described drawing as that which "evokes what is missing in what it is showing."[5] Embracing this attribute of incompleteness, this exhibition sets out an open perspective on recent drawing practices. Although the artworks reflect imaginary worlds that are representational, the exhibition's model remains a decidedly heterogeneous one. While linked, the artists' works are marked by distinctions of generation and genre, as well as by the diverse cultural genealogies underlying their

*Arteries of ink lead to brightly coloured surreal entities as the eye roams **Jason McLean**'s personal annotations on pop culture. The work has an outsider quality to it, incorporating styles and techniques gleaned from underground comics. McLean loves to discuss his bohemian, marginalized Vancouver neighbourhood, mapping places of social noteworthiness: Hendrix slept here, Ginsberg read there, Jeff Wall works here. He sees his locality as inspirational and often collaborates with other artists residing in the neighbourhood. McLean finds sustenance in the unfolding histories and new strains of narrative and myth filtering through metropolitan centres. The Final Frontier presents an anthropomorphized land/cityscape dotted with and activated by scripted speech. One is led from a lemonade stand to a pirate ship to a phone dangling a fishing hook atop a power line tower. Simultaneously one reads: "Work in your father's door factory," "You can do it in your sleep," "Lakeview Sanatorium." A dog says "Holding my hand, you look lovely today dear." McLean's medium — coloured inks — promotes mutability. He finds magic in the common and novel encounters happening in his urban environment. His conjured images and snips of dialogue reveal an enchantment with the flow between peripheral and predominant culture. For McLean, the relativity between the two feeds creativity, enlivens the imagination.*

*Selecting images of the Iraq War from the Internet, **Stephen Andrews** has reinterpreted representations of soldiers and prisoners. His use of colour separation and addition techniques, done by rubbing pastels through a screen to make dots, mimics the technology of colour television, digital pixels and screen-printing. His acts of removal and recreation produce images reminiscent of pornography and acknowledge that transference can both alter the reading of the original and magnify dormant qualities. The Quick and the Dead, a video animation, depicts an American soldier using an extinguisher to smother a burning Iraqi militiaman's body. The Iraqi was killed by a missile while bathing beside his motorcycle. Gone are any overtones of sexuality as the serviceman steps over the half-nude body to snuff the flames. Instead, as the drawings flip to manufacture the animation, the American's motions take on the quality of a stiff, macabre dance. The fluctuating specks that form the individual images are arresting; they are like smoke, a drifting pointillism. Disordered by the skill, aesthetics and technology that portray it, the Iraqi man's tragedy seems secondary. Physical and psychological distance is understood as a factor in his death and its representation.*

production. Rather than being founded on prior definitions and predetermined destinations, each piece in this exhibition has been selected to propose an instance of what drawing can be or might do. In other words, *Just My Imagination* endeavors to make a virtue of contingency, exchanging the imperative "drawing is..." for an open-ended and provisional "drawing as...." Though many pieces included here may strain the limits of traditional technical definitions of its practice, it is drawing's peculiar economy, its long-standing completion-in-incompletion, which links the various works, regardless of their material biases. Such "incompletion" can only be resolved in actively tracing the social, physical and psychic contingencies underpinning the artworks. By necessity, the critical image in *Just My Imagination* is one that is formed between the lines.

Drawing as...a Noun

The exhibition *Drawing Now* (Queens MoMA, 2002) is among recent international shows to celebrate the arrival of drawing as an independent discipline. Polemically proclaiming "drawing is a noun,"[6] curator Laura Hoptman proposed that drawing practices seen at the close of the millennium comprised a historical reversal of Richard Serra's process-championing "drawing is a verb" claim of the late 1970s. Assessing historical shifts in the tastes of collectors, her argument was phrased in a traditional opposition of finished "presentation drawings" to process-oriented "sketch" languages.[7] In her reading of the work selected for the exhibition, Hoptman argued that the present day "emancipation" of drawing derived from a reassertion of more object-centered practices, particularly those which, like academic figurative painting, privileged prior visualization, draftsmanship and finish. Though many of the characteristics and tendencies she associated with this shift can also be found in artworks included in *Just My Imagination*, her

Lucy Chan has an ongoing project of encouraging people off the street to visit her studio. While drawing their likenesses, she engages them in small talk and personal conversation. Later, she cuts and mixes this portrait with a self-portrait, switching features. She then gives the sitter one collage and keeps the other to display. A large portfolio of physical types, ages and races develops on her studio wall, accumulating into a diverse array of fanciful renditions. She titles the work Remember? We Were Close? It seems like a fluid record of humane exchange, where one is consciously or subconsciously part of many, and combinations create promising and imaginative possibilities. Another work, Lingering and Leaving, is a montage of larger drawings. In their midst is placed a miniature video screen. A number of large tubes lie on the floor in front, facing the viewer and acting as both a visual funnel and barricade. On all surfaces there are rendered images of Chan's head and torso progressing through a number of actions or slight expressions. Frequently she is alert, her eyes engage, but often she appears in a trance, dreaming. Her mediums, charcoal and ink, let her render herself as dissolving, or transparent, silhouettes walk or float through her forehead, settings, patterns, textures mesh through her body. Chan draws her physical and mental being as a channel for the recollection of encounters, sensibilities and responses.

It is difficult to retain the images that move through **David Tomas**'s digital projection. A line appears, defines a form, moves from one form to another, and then disappears, leaving only a sense of what was. Some shapes are recognizable, such as an image of a devil, while others defy exactness, such as a pictograph resembling the vertebrae and skull of a robot. Viewers may be charmed by the awakening silhouettes, entranced by the process, and may forget the earlier images until the loop repeats. In a photo-drawing series of seven works, Tomas's images are fixed yet remain indefinite. They lack the particulars of time and place, location and social context, and collapse the paradigms of scholarly disciplines. They appear delicately drawn in pencil, crayon and graphite, and mimic cave paintings, yet they reference conceptualism and minimalism. Some seem art historically connected — a geometric rendition of a simian imitates Picasso's cubist baboon. Although they look like drawings, they are lambda prints on aluminium, the originals technologically processed and aestheticized. Their infinite white grounds are mirrors. In one, a parachutist falls directly into an ellipse. The ellipse suggests completeness. It has a defined centre and can be imagined as a flattened eye in perspective. The parachutist passes through and fractures, his remains scattered below. Tomas is interested in displacement.[1] He uses the dissolution of borders — between mediums, symbols, disciplines, and time — to envision a transformative space where movement and exchange are desired conditions. By exhibiting digital prints of the drawings, he removes tactility and minimizes materiality.

polemic would appear to discount the continuing, and in many cases, reconfigured, role which process plays in both the artists' production and audience reception of recent drawing-based work. It also neatly brackets out the disciplinary crossovers that have long characterized drawing and have become second nature to contemporary artists' practices. To return once more to the linguistic analogy, if "drawing is a noun," then *Just My Imagination* attempts to restore the structural role which "verbs" need to play, before completing any sentence on drawing.

Just My Imagination

Aligned with either the object-sense of the presentation drawing or the process-sense of the sketch, each work in this exhibition has been consciously produced as a self-sufficient entity. Whether operating on a material, technical or conceptual level, all these works reflect a rigorous, if at times provocative, relationship with drawing traditions. While most artists work on paper, few choose to restrict their practice to this ground alone. Some actively transfer the conventions of drawing into other media, while others deliberately cross disparate formal languages to confound media categories altogether. In their range, these works encompass both pre-visualized approaches and those born of more open ends: some make visible the material conditions of their making, while others are inclined to secret this making within themselves; some consist of unique works on paper, while others work to exploit drawing's transferability or reproducibility. In all these works, drawing can be seen offering a nimble, highly adaptable language — one exceptionally well tooled to visualizing processes of thought. And in tracing successive displacements of thought, the resulting artworks may appear logical and coherent or disjointed and wandering. Regardless of their path, the imaginary spaces that emerge in *Just My Imagination* are typically complex: crowded,

A large, veiled core is suspended by appendages attached to walls and floor-to-ceiling fibre cables. Images of rising waves are sewn into its transparent silk skin. Naturally dark wool gathers into felt, forms organic shapes or moves along the arms. This artwork looks like sculpture but impersonates drawing. **Luanne Martineau** *calls it "drulpture." To make felt, she has repeatedly punched the yarn together with a needle, eventually making it so strong that it cannot be torn apart. The needle functions here like a pencil; numerous gestures build up to form mass. The running lines of yarn seem to channel energy. The supports define margins by specifying distances. The spaces between the points where these limbs touch the walls and where they attach to the screened surface converge inversely, indicating a linear, interior perspective. This membrane, an embodied capacity, is lined with swells and surges. It considered, marks and casts the conscious and unconscious.*

In tall, tunnel-like installations outfitted with portals opening to inner sanctums, or in small intense drawings, **Ed Pien** *depicts multi-eyed children, demon squid and bestial mutants, all with grasping, penetrating tentacles. Swimming in seas of ink-stained paper, the beings are often constructed by overlaying different mythical creatures. A favourite, stemming from Pien's heritage, is a Chinese water ghost perpetually enticing the living into re-enacting its own fate, death by drowning. Monsters can be analogs for anxieties related to insecurities, overindulgence, self-absorption and soulless acts of depletion. Pien's hauntings seem polarized — beautifully wrought and not necessarily frightening. A terrible infant is still guileless, even as it experiences its first yearnings and hungers. In "Against Interpretation," Susan Sontag wrote about the critical importance of seeing, feeling and hearing more.[2] The multiple eyes and flexible organs of Pien's entities imply an intense need for emotional, sensory and cerebral nourishment. Need and use are commensurate with growth, and to flourish, one must learn from one's fears.*

overlaid, discontinuous. Repeatedly, familiar figurative form is given to slip, its markers uncoupling and re-coupling in unanticipated and often unsettling ways. In the resulting encounter, every detail appears to unfold as a psychic event — one perpetually perched on the edge of becoming something else.

Commuting Sentences

Developing out of drawing's traditional embrace of the ephemeral, all the works in this exhibition reflect a condition of temporal volatility. This shows itself in several ways. Most familiarly, it appears in the precarious materiality of drawing, or, through the sensual language of the trace, in its immediacy to the actions involved in its making. In *Just My Imagination* this volatility can also be seen extending to the artwork's imagery. The image world rendered here is a changing one, where contradictions coexist and conditions of transformation appear a norm. Frequently deriving from automatic, diaristic or repetitive processes, additive procedures underlie much of these works' production. In this approach, discrete elements have a tendency to proliferate and accumulate, yielding aggregate forms that can readily build to physically immersive scales. Echoing cinematic conditions of "perception in the state of distraction," viewers must often contend with an inability to instantly grasp the contents of the resulting works. Responding in kind, the viewer's engagement is made subject to conditions of duration as well. This engagement may evolve on the spot, in a restless probing of details, or in a more fully embodied way, unfolding in step with the physical movement required to experience the more expansive works. It is not surprising that, in embracing such temporalized conditions, some artists in this exhibition have come to extend their drawing practice into actual time-based media. In these explicitly mobilized works, discrete images are reassembled linearly, in the form of stop-

Cathy Daley is known for using gestured drawing to depict oversized icons of female apparel. Her renditions of ample dresses, elongated stockings and stiletto shoes suggest they are living things, anthropomorphized entities. Occasionally she has translated them into fibre sculptures. The energy of the massed lines and the exaggerated shapes of these garments evoke a presence that playfully censures the limitations enforced by conventional gendered appearances. In Just My Imagination, she exhibits twenty-two drawings of various sizes, each depicting the same lightly drawn fluffy crinolines moving on top of stocking legs. Individually framed and hung in a group, they rise forty feet on the wall. They seem like a bizarre mass ascension, a bank of gently swelling clouds, a floating throng of gyrating can-can outfits. A paradox, mesmerizing to behold, they critique the canonization of fantastical sexual stereotypes.

In Draw Me a Monster: Bestiary III *Anna Torma* has taken her young son's drawings of creatures and apocalypses and, through cutting and stitching, copied them into quilts. Behind and around these monsters are sewn learning charts, numerical scales, words associated with various occupations, and colours connected to certain animals. Torma understands that learning and invention should be intertwined. Her approach emphatically acknowledges the arbitrary relationship between naïve, unsettling fantasies and the joys of imagining. Yet her use of a medium linked with domesticity and comfort reduces the malignancy of, even beautifies, the imagery. The immeasurable threading evidences the patience necessary both to produce her work and to cultivate creative intelligence. In a second piece, Draw Me a Car shapes are smaller, sparser and visually less concrete: flowers, plants, cells, hearts, car logos and peace signs. Lines are muted or overlap, and build in numbers. Here it appears energy is massing and sensibilities are forming.

frame animations, as well as non-linearly, in programmed or interactive digital forms. If, as Bill Viola has suggested, the contemporary image is a temporary image, the present relevance of drawing would seem hardly diminished.[8] Irrespective of the media or processes employed by its artists, in *Just My Imagination*, the work appears to happen in the process of looking at it.

The End Is Not the End

In embracing both newly developed and formerly marginalized visual languages, the drawing-based works in *Just My Imagination* reflect a disciplinary complexity that has become the common terrain of contemporary artists' practices. However, despite the recent shifts in tactics and the growing institutional recognition of drawing, it would be a mistake to conclude that its present strength is at a great remove from its traditional roles and approaches. The current championing of drawing as an autonomous practice is clearly rooted in its long-standing robustness — both as a discipline in itself, and potentially, in others. Regardless of the inevitable shifts in visual art's discourses, trends and technologies, drawing will continue to provide artists the immediate tools of visual thinking and communication it always has. It will also continue to be valued as a legitimate and self-sustaining basis of ambitious artistic practices. But in the end, perhaps it is unproductive to belabour the question of whether drawing has finally been granted its own high office or whether it is merely enjoying a well-earned fifteen minutes in the sun. In both traditional function and vision, drawing has always been wedded to the future, to the emergent, to the virtual, to the yet known. Like the best of contemporary art, to making the unimaginable imaginable.

David Merritt

Animals, clothing, infants, puppets, walking penises and whimsical texts coexist in **Candice Tarnowski**'s *intuitive drawing. They envision an alternative space where the divisions between subject and object, the primacies of gender and species, have collapsed. In their place, crossbred entities facilitate balance and parity. For* Just My Imagination, *an unnamed work is installed that consists of nine distinct sections. Three small drawings are hung one above another and then horizontally aligned with three small dioramas and three large photographs. The pencil crayon drawings are representational and symbolic. In the dioramas, figures from the drawings become tiny polymer characters nestled in settings constructed from fibres, yarn and wool. The photographs demonstrate that the matter of construction can change again, as small flower buds and plant stems are used to represent the aligned preceding images. Most of the nine sections seem to reference a stage, with curtains or containing walls. But an analysis of the scene and its implied story depends as much upon a response to the materials of construction as to its imagery. Tarnowski's hybrids dissolve some boundaries of elemental and type hierarchies and question how formulated translations can determine values.*

Sheila Butler *has created an installation in which a high, seventy-five-foot wall of transparent fabric meanders across the gallery then trails to the ground. Drawn on this veil are large arms and hands reaching out, as well as sleeping heads. A stretch of paper is visible behind the veil; it extends around a corner on the wall. Its surface features faces both cognizant and turned away, and sections of falling male bodies. Some of the smaller heads look like representations of a manicured woman from the 1950s. Collaged at the top of the paper are heavy work gloves, some painted with the same woman's hair and face. A line of text splits the length of the paper. It describes one of the artist's dreams — at an opening Butler encounters a man whose looks she finds disturbing, he resembles a biker. This work can be interpreted as a dream about identity, the painted gloves an affirmation of Butler's artist persona, or as psychoanalytic investigation of gender issues, the housewife a stereotype of the conventions of her youth. But the gallery is a physical space and, depending on where one stands, it is possible to view a range of symbols behind the images on the transparent barrier, creating a shifting psychic mix that involves both genders. Butler has produced drawings where people give and receive mouth-to-mouth resuscitation or expel clouds of air. They can be read as communions, acts of consumption, or exorcisms. When forging or sustaining a sense of self, it is inherently necessary to deal with social strictures, personal conditioning, and conjectures made about others. A high winding wall then ends and cascades down.*

Kim Moodie

[Notes]

David Merritt

1. Michel Serres, "The Origin of Language," in *Hermes, Literature, Science, Philosophy* (Baltimore: John Hopkins University Press, 1983), 75. The image Serres offers in this quote was originally made in comparing living organisms and information systems.

2. John Berger, "To Take Paper and Draw," *Harpers Magazine* (September 1990): 57–60.

3. Paul Klee, in *Notebooks, Volume 1: The Thinking Eye*, ed. Jürg Spiller, trans. Ralph Mannheim (London: Lund Humphries,1961), 169.

4. A presentation drawing is customarily considered a "finished" drawing, one that is complete in itself. Usually representing the final stage of development of an artist's idea prior to being translated into another medium, historically such drawings were often offered as a gift to the artist's patron.

5. Hubert Damisch, *A Theory of /Cloud/: Toward a History of Painting*, trans. Janet Lloyd (Stanford: Stanford University Press, 2002), 130. Damisch's original comment was made in the context of examining the role of line in writing in relation to its role in drawing and painting.

6. Barbara Hoptman, *Drawing Now: Eight Propositions* (New York: Museum of Modern Art, 2002), 11–12.

7. Written from the perspective of a collecting institution, it is not surprising Hoptman's assessment proceeds from an account of historical patterns of collecting, nor that MoMA's criteria for drawing (unique works on paper) would appear to circumscribe her selection of works for the exhibition.

8. Bill Viola, "Video Black – The Mortality of the Image," in *Reasons for Knocking at an Empty House* (Cambridge: MIT Press, 1995), 202–209.

Kim Moodie

1. Michèle Thèriault, "Transduction of Knowledge, Psychasthenia of Media," Michèle Thèriault, David Tomas, *Duction*. (Artist's book, Editions Carapace: Montreal, Quebec, 2001), 65-67.

2. Susan Sontag, "Against Interpretation," in *Against Interpretation*. (Farrar, Straus & Giroux: New York, 1969), 14.

David Merritt and **Kim Moodie** are drawing-based artists who teach at the University of Western Ontario in London, Canada.

Jason McLean, *The Final Frontier,* 2004 (detail)

Just My Imagination?

[Kym Pruesse]

DRAWING. Such a primary, immediate thing. How strange that it is so difficult to write about... I circumscribe, travel around, narrow down, but miss. The missing seems right in the end. But sharing the journey is important, so I imagine a gesture in-between writing and drawing — a diary of thoughts triggered by the art in this exhibition.

My sister and I are driving to Nanaimo. I notice on the map that there are petroglyphs at a park on the way. A perfect picnic spot. The trail is short and ends at a lookout facing a sheer cliff bearing the petroglyphs. They are so direct, intentional. I wonder why the park doesn't have an interpretation. These beautiful, animated drawings of sea creatures seem to say that the squiggly river we had been following will give way to the ocean, just beyond the lake we are picnicking on.

When we return to the car, I check the map again to see if these drawings are the road signs I imagined. Indeed, the local harbour does lead to the sea, perhaps one of the most unexpected inland connections in Canada. I can't confirm my interpretation, but I do know that I had a profound moment of looking and listening to the past and it spoke to me through time. What also intrigued me was the characterization of the creatures. Not monstrous, but definitely haunting. So I think I discovered something about the people who drew them — their awe of the sea and the importance of the transition from fresh to salt water.

I know this anecdote is an indirect way of speaking about an art exhibition, but the petroglyphs reminded me that each discovery is always a rediscovery. When we do this thing called art, we never know what will survive, what will speak, what will make sense to future generations. All we can really do is point others in the direction of our fascination.

During a studio visit with **Ed Pien**, we speak about his fascination with ghosts, or at least the representation of ghosts, witches, and the spirit world. He talks about the psychological function of such images as the externalization of fear. They capture the liminal stuff at the core of our being. Yet what is also curious is that his images are shape-shifters; they mutate into animals, grow extra limbs, become grotesque. Both human and not-human, his creatures personify the meeting ground of the conscious mind with the unconscious. His drawing method involves spontaneous doodles and accidents of ink that he then develops into characters with complex mythologies. In his recent work, the drawings have taken dimensional form as installations. Or, as I like to think, they create a domain...a life of their own. Pien's exploration of both old and new traditions is a reminder of what we already know but may have become too comfortable with.... Perhaps that is the importance of shape-shifting; it makes the familiar odd and full of unexpected potential.

Sheila Butler's work is informed by years of academic training, teaching, as well as profound exchanges with Canada's northern indigenous communities, but her practice consistently trespasses conventions. Her area of exploration demands a breaching of the known: How can the world of dreams, inchoate drives and memories be visualized and given validity? *Essential Tremor* is a long, floating meditation on dreams, association and the science of it — psychoanalysis. As a drawing installation, the work places space, line, volume, text and the viewer in relation to each other in a manner that is both awkward and beautiful. Personal references blend with cultural signifiers and overt objectness (a glove, silky textiles, words, drawings on paper) to produce a space of contemplation. Human experience can be full of unanswered questions, yearnings, disjunctive memories and unresolved tensions, but that is also part of its joy. Butler's work rests within this fragile territory. Not fearing the un-endingness of the journey, she calls on us to both experience it and celebrate it.

Being witness to inner and outer worlds is one of the threads that weaves through this exhibition.

An artist with a kaleidoscopic profile, **Jason McLean** is an illustrator, designer, sculptor, innovator, performer and collaborator in cultural interventions. Known for his work with *Adbusters* and 'zine culture, McLean is never far from the pulse of popular culture. His sensitivity to outsider views makes me look at his work with sympathy and curiosity. These quirky, surreal maps of his neighbourhood chart a psychological landscape filled with real but fictional characters. The mapping is intriguing and playful, yet his pictures beg the question of how we "know" a place. While McLean's portraits of his immediate world may expose as much about him as his environment, they are also invitations to view the world in new ways. I am led to imagine my own neighbourhood. His diagrammatic interpretations of social interaction, or lack thereof, speaks volumes about how we are evolving as a society. The spirit of the work is kind but precise. It is truthful. I want him to be a politician. Maybe he already is.

I see great visual variety in this exhibition, even a challenge to the traditions of drawing. What I am drawn to, however, is the their dark invitation…seductive and at the same time sinister.

Cathy Daley ruminates about popular representations of women — those sexy, highly polished images we see in advertising, fashion magazines, fairy-tales and cartoons. What comes to mind is the collective masquerade of the female body. Which images inform our fantasies of beauty? What do we do to ourselves to try to look like that? Daley's black-and-white drawings and sculptures exaggerate limbs and body parts — parts accessorized with fashion heels, puffy skirts, fishnet stockings, etc. Blown out of proportion and fragmented, these remanipulated bodies foreground other levels of social manipulation. It's not that the resulting images are demonic, didactic or even overtly political, but they do become funny in a troubling way. Daley isolates the trouble and scrutinizes it in a plush visual form. In counterpoint to the wizardry of airbrushed mass media, Daley's images are minimal and somewhat mournful. Black pastel on long sheets of translucent vellum, brash sweeps of line, volume aided by liquidy solvents. So simple, so concise, so profound.

I want to write concisely, but feel that much is left unsaid. What does it mean to admit that one can only gesture towards the truth? Perhaps the most meaningful things lie in the pauses, the gaps, the unstated in-betweens. In the end it is really about the encounter. It is up to each of us to find a connection in our own way, on our own terms.

Pushing at boundaries, and thinking through connectivity, lie at the heart of **Michelle Gay**'s creative enterprise. Her studio is full of eerily beautiful ink drawings, but also computers (five at my last visit), all powered by hard-drives she built herself. Gay's practice transcends genres by weaving together old-fashioned get-down-and-draw with twenty-first-century technology. A sense of play permeates the work. In one digital projection, two figures (one a scanned ink drawing from her wall, the other a morphed image of Gay's head on a drawn body with winged flaps) are attached to strings like bungee chords. The characters gleefully bounce around in a virtual dance designed to respond to the random interaction of each other and the viewer's intervention. As Gay blurs the categories of drawing, photography and digital imaging, the work poses questions about "interactivity": To what extent is art interactive and collective? Does technology bring real time and individual presence into art? But it is not the technology that presides; it is Gay's universe of weird characters, involved in elusive endeavours, that captures the imagination.

I find myself seduced by the suggestion of things that cannot be caught in the web of logic. In all these works, there is a gesture toward what cannot be drawn or spoken, but somehow known.

Stephen Andrews gleans his source images from the Internet, yet they are ominously reminiscent of Goya's nineteenth-century dedication to the *Disasters of War*: scenes of torture, death and unfathomable degradation. How do we make sense of these images? Or do we give up? Are we complacent and therefore complicit? Andrews' labour-intensive process of transferring the digital images into hand-separated colour matrices provides distance and room for contemplation. The work does not feel exploitative; it is compassionate, sorrowful, empathetic, yet also confusing. How does one ask profound questions in crayon? Then there are his animation stills and web-link pop-ups, which point to the strange flattening effect of contemporary media. As Andrews reduces the technologies of communication to their basics, he also foregrounds their psychological and emotional emptiness. The artist speaks of the "failure" of the hand. I think he is describing his effort to capture elusive moments of history, like ours, now, in pictures. But it is not the hand that fails; we fail ourselves by not taking notice of what is going on around us.

John Scott has worked with paper, paint, sculpture and contemporary mindscapes for a long time. Views of war, war machines and eccentric characters (like the distressed "bunny-sapiens") are recurring themes. Dystopian? Maybe, but there is a redemptive quality, a deep care for how images of war have made us apathetic. Scott provides fruitful musings about how we collaborate with popular media to reproduce a dysfunctional cultural imagination. Some recent drawings feature a motorcycle rigged up to twirl industrial drums with ancient prayers locked inside, a reference to Tibetan prayer wheels. My memories from Nepal are of old women walking mountainous trails spinning small hand-held prayer wheels. Each spin sends a prayer out into the universe. Larger drums are often affixed around the perimeter of stupas (round Buddhist structures) so that circling pilgrims can spin them for good will. I imagine Scott's motor-driven wheels accelerating the spin into a panicked frenzy. Potentially ominous and loud, they evoke a contemporary translation of hope tinged with distress.

As a child, I remember being confused about certain images: the crucified Christ in plastic-coated living rooms; colourful Hindu gods strung with flowers on the dashboard of a bus; scary shamanic masks in the calm atmosphere of museums. Fear and death are implied, but most of all there is transformation – the movement from the known to the unknown. Just enough detail to make us associate, just enough mystery to disassociate. In that oscillation, I am compelled to ask: What is it that I want from these pictures?

David Tomas begins with drawing, but doesn't always end with it, or does he? Tomas investigates the transformations that occur when drawings are mapped onto other technologies. Previously, he has produced an interactive virtual reality program that combines references to two historical buildings in London: the Camden Roundhouse (an engine house for rerouting trains built in 1846), and the circular Reading Room of the British Museum (from 1857, now relocated). Integrated into the program is a pathway based on the first architectural sketch of the Reading Room and sound elements that reference the artist's memory of rock concerts held in the Roundhouse during the 1960s and 1970s. The two round buildings are aligned by their function as innovative solutions for storage and retrieval (trains, books) — much like the function of computers and the world-wide web today. But the work is also an experiment with the tracing of space and memory, and the convergence of media within the larger context of understanding the control of technology, or perhaps the "technology of control." We must not forget that drawing, too, is a technology.

Another similarity in the artworks here is the exploration of media. No terrain, no form of technology, is off limits. How has the development of technology changed our ways of seeing and knowing? The questions I am led to are both cerebral and phenomenological.

Luanne Martineau draws but also utilizes textiles to produce what she calls "drulptures": artworks that are part-drawing, part-sculpture. The braiding, felting and drawing techniques result in a hairy tent-like structure with long "dreadlock" extensions. The work is a little menacing. Its knobbly tentacles reach out into the viewer's space. Yet the natural fibres make the work feel somewhat benign – it is soft, after all. Oozy, squooshy, spatial and lateral, there is a curious repulsion and seduction, a desire to touch and a fear of getting too close. Some viewers may be overwhelmed by its sculptural presence and wonder how it is a "drawing." Others may approach the work intuitively, feeling and making personal associations. My thoughts go to memories of swimming in unfamiliar lakes and oceans, not knowing what slimy strands of seaweed might curl around my legs. The sea has long been a metaphoric repository for the unconscious. Martineau's fibrous housing seems like a magnet for the unformed yet latent uncertainties we all drag with us.

Lucie Chan deals with the fragile and fascinating notion of identity. How do we construct a sense of self? How does that differ from what others perceive? To explore these questions, Chan invites people to have their portraits drawn. Portraits are arguably the most sensitive things to look at. All one's personal details, both on the surface and beneath, become the subject of attention. Chan then draws another portrait — a composite of herself and the sitter. What we see in the exhibit are the hybrid faces. Some are rolled into tubes, others hang on the wall, but all seem to be whispering their lives and stories. One can't help but wonder if in the differences and similarities there is a longing for the things that unite rather than divide. I find myself filling in the dialogue between the faces, between self and other, self and self. Chan's video animations evoke a similar sense of disconnect and desire. Slow blinking eyes in close-cropped outlines of heads that never merge...moving drawings that tell tales of effort and reach, arriving finally at us — like the initial portraits that she returns to her volunteers.

In drawing we invent symbols, we invent communication. Of all the possible forms of language, drawing links us most strongly to the dawn of our efforts to speak to each other.

Raphaëlle de Groot's projects are context-driven. She calls them "field investigations": information collected through a rhythm of encounters and interactions with a specific community (e.g., nuns, the blind, domestic workers). For this exhibition, de Groot worked out of an artist-in-residence program in London, ON. As I look over her past projects, I am struck by the consistency of her interest in trace narratives, untold stories and marginal social experiences. She immerses herself in a location, gathering evidence of presence, work and lifestyle, and then transforms it through the labour of art-making. The resulting work is inhabited by a deep respect for lives lived with heroic intensity, but not always understood by dominant culture. She is able to translate the heartfelt endeavours of a community into a visual language that captures both its vulnerabilities and unique sensitivities. Yet, as a viewer, I find myself strangely cared for. Are *we*, perhaps, the subject of her inquiry as well?

I have never thought of art as arriving at an answer, a truth. For me, art is about the impulse to probe. But there are times when things coalesce — like a dragonfly resting on your knee in a field of grass, such fleetingly yet unfathomable beauty. How do we express that convergence of the momentary and the lasting? Perhaps one way is to chart small things and hope they give way to a larger picture. This might explain the diaristic compulsion of many artists, a need to take notice of the day to day...to give it attention, expand our experience of it.

Candice Tarnowski is a diarist. She takes note of daily routines, journals them, and draws them into ethereal dreamscapes. The drawings float with animal and human characters who come and go, except for the ever-present wormy things (representing the audience? witnesses? the artist?). These intimately-scaled musings are later transformed into three-dimensional form, molded from animal hair, clay and found objects. There is an odd sense of perspective, an homage to specifics, such as when one tries to recall a dream. In that fluttering moment between sleeping and wakefulness, remnants of the unconscious are caught in the act of looking. This meeting place of images, thoughts and feelings is difficult to translate, which may be why Tarnowski then photographs the work — another gesture toward bringing the inside out in order to ponder its reality. Tarnowski's invitation to share her process of introspection feels like a gentle but focused caress: a place to rest and gather insight.

The movement from two- to three-dimensions, and then back again, is a process consistent throughout this exhibition. There is also the translation of size that I find compelling. It's as if intimacy, comfort, and the presence of the viewer are under examination.

Looking at **Alison Norlen**'s large-scale charcoal and chalk drawings, I see a tilted wedge of abstract space crammed with a frenetic flood of information. In an age bombarded with infomercials, channel surfing, news images and web ads, it makes sense that someone would try to capture its compression and oppression. In the quiet of the gallery, though, I appreciate the compositional rhythms and intuit the strange worlds of Bosch and Dali, as well as Las Vegas, Disneyland and New York after 9/11. The squished, rambunctious spatial plane makes me think of Bakhtin's writing about carnivals and the carnivalesque — that short time when chaos rules and repressed fantasies are played out. Are we in perpetual carnival today? All glitter on the surface but dingy and carnal underneath? Norlen's pictures serve up both the shine and tarnish of contemporary cultural facades. Yet there are also odd interjections of rural life: a wood stove, wheat sheaves, a modest wood-frame house, pumpkins and cattle. As a juxtaposition of realities, these monumental drawings reveal the tenuous scaffolding of a swiftly changing world.

Anna Torma's embroidered drawings resonate with skill but also with a sympathy for what we tend not to think of as high art. Her work fuses a child's naïf aesthetic with the knowledge of tradition, history, art and craft. There are references to illuminated manuscripts, medieval cosmologies, bestiaries (pictures and tales of phantasmatic animals), symbols from indigenous cultures and, most obviously, children's drawings of monsters and soldiers of the night — those creatures untethered by the limitations of the real. Torma has translated these into textile, layered with narrative and stitches, and done with an idiosyncratic sense of composition. Her work recalls palimpsests, those recycled documents used over and over when materials were scarce. They reflect a dedicated touch that reaches into a larger cultural history of capturing the imagination. They are whimsical, intricate studies imbued with a disarming freshness and invitation to pleasure.

Just My Imagination celebrates drawing, in both its simplicity and complexity, as a primordial site for marking and bridging states of transformation. The ability to make sense of a world full of confusing images is especially important today. These artists ask us to give pause to our visual consumption. While contemporary in production, content and media, there is a legacy of effort that is as ancient as the petroglyphs.... Whatever the result, the point of departure is something very basic: the act of mark-making and the desire to evidence a journey. But that is not all that draws us in. It is also the internal issues, the soul's search for external membership in the world.

Art is a circular path of sorts, so I will end where I began — on a journey with a map. I stand before an ancient set of drawings that point to another world and the transition between. I don't know much about the territory, but I want to follow it. The works here speak to the travels of the human psyche and ask us to share it with them. Let's listen and enjoy the gift.

The Quick and the Dead, 2004

The Quick and the Dead, 2004 (video stills Photo: Stephen Andrews)

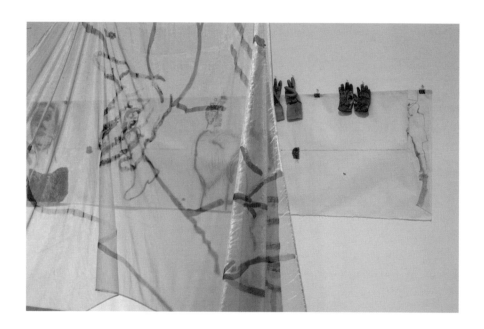

above: *Study for Breathing in the Cold*, 2003 (left) and *Essential Tremor,* 2002 (right)

opposite: *Essential Tremor,* 2002 (detail)

John Scott and Team Apocalypse, *Substitute for the Prayer Wheel,* 2004 (detail)

Recording the World – Drawing Today

[Daina Augaitis]

AT A TIME WHEN PHOTOGRAPHY AND VIDEO are the dominant forms garnering the attention of collectors and saturating the discourses of the museum, it is interesting that the old-fashioned art of drawing has emerged as a popular alternative, sneaking in as an antidote to the cool, slick surfaces of highly produced art. Artists themselves are often the first to react to the popular and the overused, steering away from well-trodden paths in order to explore unknown margins or to revisit the old with renewed enthusiasm. Increasing numbers of contemporary artists use the humble and handy medium of paper and pencil, which allows for a rule-defying and liberating do-it-yourself approach.

What's different about drawing today? Drawing has always represented directness, communicating an uninterrupted flow from the cerebral or emotional interior to the external world. It captures the physical gesture of the hand, carrying with it a message from the centre. In a world where communications are mediated by BlackBerries and cell phones, the raw, direct mark-making of a drawing is endearing, almost quaint, offering a physical concreteness and suggesting a slower, more considered pace in the face of life lived at high-tech speed. Whether they are an escape from a dysfunctional world or a critique of our social landscapes, today's drawings are largely representational, and the frenzied conditions of contemporary life are not lost on artists who engage in drawing-based practices. In fact there is an obsessive quality to many contemporary drawings: some embody the passage of time through visible, smeary erasures; others rely on naïve depictions of the vernacular of pop culture; the perfect polish of still others brings surreal visions to life. Artists are making use of the intimacy of drawing not just to explore the personal but also to uncover fragments of a larger cultural unconscious and to redress some of today's impersonal encounters.

above/right:
Lingering and Leaving, 2004
(detail/installation view)

opposite:
Remember? We Were Close? 2004
(detail)

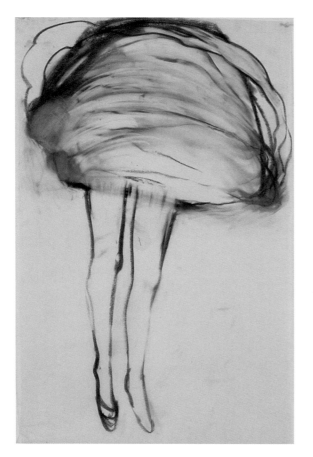

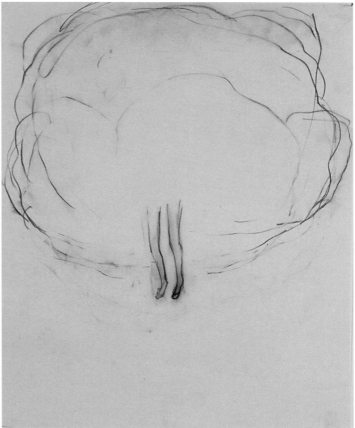

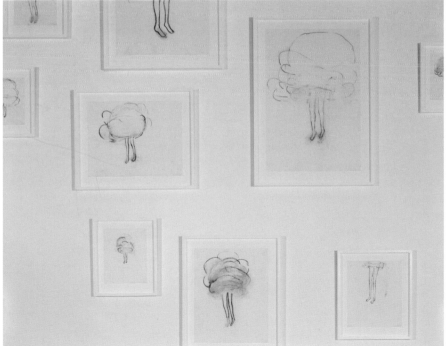

rise/fall, 2004 (installation view/details)

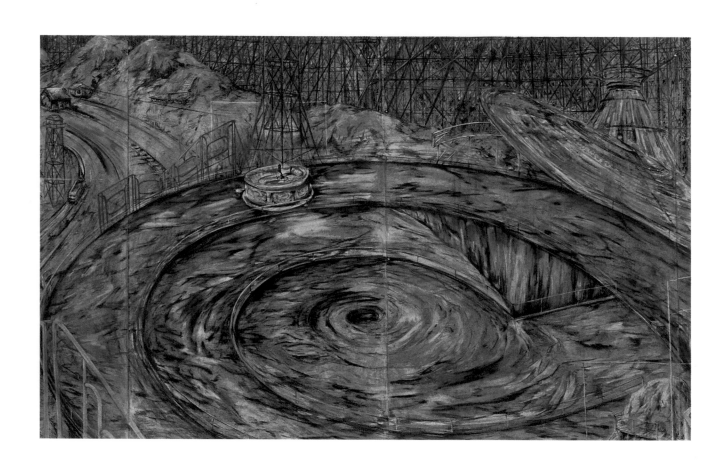

Alison Norlen, *Untitled*, 2004 (detail)

Moving on Drawing

[Cliff Eyland]

A STATEMENT BY ROBERT KUDIELKA in a 1972 interview with Bridget Riley provides a measure of drawing's slow climb to importance over the past thirty years. Kudielka called Riley one of the "few artists today who make preliminary studies."[1] So many of today's artists begin and end their practice in "preliminary studies" that Kudielka's suggestion produces a mild shock at first reading.

This latest drawing revolution should not have happened, at least according to the logic of fads: we are supposed to be in the era of digital art in which work is done by the hand only if scanning is impossible. Distressingly, for some, contemporary original drawings position digital media as mere documentation that must always to be authenticated by the presence of something "real."

Drawing has thrived in Winnipeg because it is the town that Conceptual Art forgot. Artists never stopped drawing and the local art school has never wavered in its enthusiasm for drawing instruction. With the exception of Jeff Funnell, who teaches at the University of Manitoba School of Art, conceptual artists who matured in Winnipeg — for example, Gordon LeBredt and General Idea's Felix Partz — left town. Hence when drawing came back big in the early 1990s, Winnipeg was well-positioned to export drawings not only by Marcel Dzama and The Royal Art Lodge, but also many others: established artists such as Wanda Koop, Ivan Eyre, Richard Williams, Diane Thorneycroft and Derek Brueckner; Art Lodge contemporaries such as Jake Kosiuk and Simon Hughes; and emerging artists such as Shaun Morin, Erica Eyres and Cyrus Smith.

Drawing may be back for good (full disclosure: I myself draw every day), but we may be nearing the end of the line for post-adolescent drawing that flaunts its abjectness and authenticity like stigmata. Celebrations like the The Royal Art Lodge's much-lauded and well-attended 2003 show at The Drawing Center in New York will not likely be repeated since the Lodge, not to mention other maturing collectives, tend to break up as their members become individually successful. And success, as we know, can make authenticity into a suspicious set of representations. As for abjection — at least apropos art school trained artists — that joke is best told by very smart people like Mike Kelley and not (however smart they really are) by young art collectives.

We need to draw on, but also need to move on.

Note

1. Robert Kudielka, "Bridget Riley in Conversation with Robert Kudielka," in Paul Moorehouse, ed., *Bridget Riley* (London: Tate, 2003), 208.

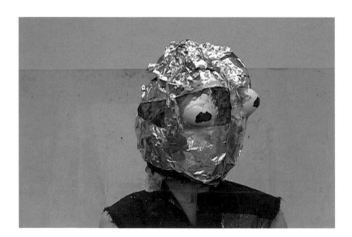

performance stills
Photos: Mirko Sabatini

Third Person, Drawing session at the University of Western Ontario, 2004 (installation view)

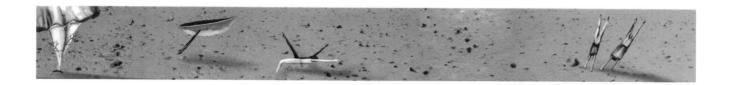

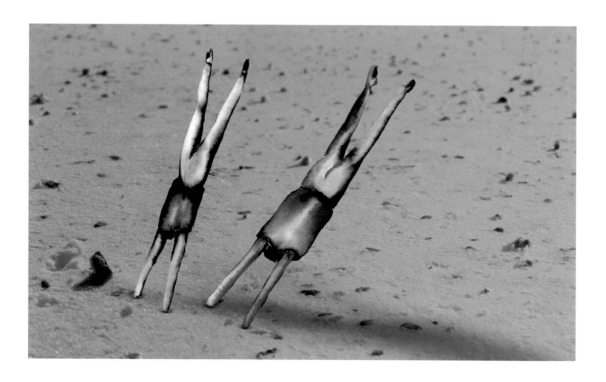

Cels from an Epic, 2004 Photos: Michelle Gay

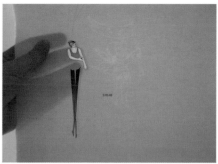

top: *Swat* and *The Studio* (from the *Seuss Faces the Abyss* suite), 2003 (installation view)

bottom: *The Studio* (from the *Seuss Faces the Abyss* suite), 2003 (detail) Photo: Michelle Gay

Luanne Martineau, *Untitled*, 2004

The Moving Finger

[Robin Metcalfe]

WHAT IS A DRAWING? No definition will separate it cleanly from painting, writing or dance. It usually deals with line, edge and boundary rather than colour, area or mass. It is dry (like graphite) or thin (like ink) rather than thick and wet like paint. Classically, it achieves its final form immediately upon contact with the support, which is presumptively paper. It is image rather than word, a distinction nevertheless blurred in Islamic and Oriental calligraphic traditions. It records the body's movement but it is not that movement itself.

Two streams of practice appear among younger artists who draw. One, fusing conceptual and formalist traditions, focuses on the gesture of drawing, the mechanics of draughtsmanship, reduced to its purist simplicity and repeated or extended to an obsessive, potentially absurd, degree. The works of Kelly Mark and Lucy Pullen, both educated at the Nova Scotia College of Art and Design, demonstrate this approach.

The other stream concerns itself with image content, by way of the cartoon, as popularly understood: an expressive drawing, usually of figures, often ephemeral and off-hand. It shrugs off the classical tradition of virtuoso draughtsmanship, which seems beside the point in the wake of photography and digital imagery. Instead, it focuses on imaginative and psychological content, a self-deprecating disclosure of the contents of the unconscious that owes as much to Surrealism as to the funny papers. The Royal Art Lodge and Shary Boyle provide instances of this, as does the line based printmaking of Julie Voyce.

Both streams meet at their source, the older meaning of cartoon. "Cartoon" derives from *cartone*, cardboard, originally from the Latin term *charta*, a leaf of papyrus. It means a drawing on paper that is the plan for, and the same size as, a fresco, mosaic or tapestry.

A handmaiden to more heroic practices, drawing has been the uniquely indispensable technical skill of all visual art. The preparatory drawing (from life, still life or landscape) mediates between the world-as-seen and the world-as-represented in a painting, sculpture or building. Recording visual experience in the most objective mode (as in a topographical drawing) or serving as the armature for a visual experience yet to be created, drawing was for a long time the most precise visual tool to render worlds as they are or might be. Photography partly supplanted classical media. Now the computer has brought photography to the condition of drawing or painting — an exercise of the moving hand.

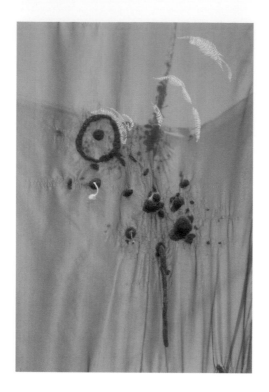

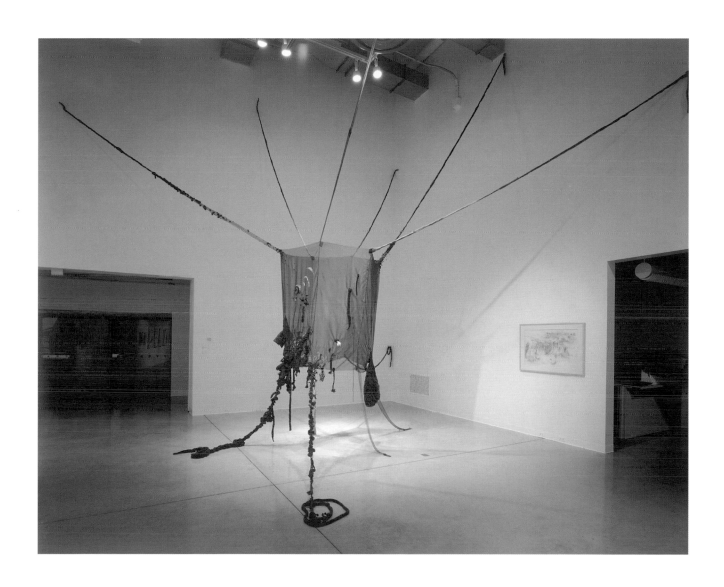

above: *Parasite,* 2004 (installation view)
left: *Parasite,* 2004 (details)

The Final Frontier, 2004

The Valley Beneath the Sun, 2004

Contemporary Drawing Practices

[David Liss]

I HAVE ALWAYS BEEN INSPIRED by Paul Klee's notion that drawing is like taking a line for a walk — a notion that suggests habit, adventure, discovery. Drawing can be an invigorating activity good for the body and soul, or, just as easily, a mundane or leisurely routine with no particular accomplishment in mind.

From pictographic cave images to digital-age drawings, mark-making has always been present. Interestingly, however, it has never been considered particularly fashionable or commercially viable.

Drawing is often the genesis of great ideas and can also be a finished product of great sophistication. At its very essence it requires nothing more than a rudimentary tool and the human imagination. As it is clear in this exhibition, in contemporary artistic practice a drawing can be a single, independent artwork, large or small; it can be combined with other materials; or it can be a component of a serial production or an installation.

Within the last couple of decades drawing has been taken more seriously. A number of exhibitions have sought to explore the boundaries of drawing and to garner wider respect for the medium. I am not convinced, however, that such motivations are necessary. Over the course of time it seems that the context for drawing has not changed significantly. I interpret this as a good thing. It exists outside of temporal mainstream tastes and resists becoming a full-fledged commodity. Drawing, by its very nature, has always been persistent in the imagination of the artist. It remains the intimate, even sacred, territory of their unbound imagination. It's just artists' imaginations, runnin' away, runnin' away...

David Tomas, *Untitled*, 2004 Photo: David Tomas

Alison Norlen, *Untitled*, 2004 (detail left)

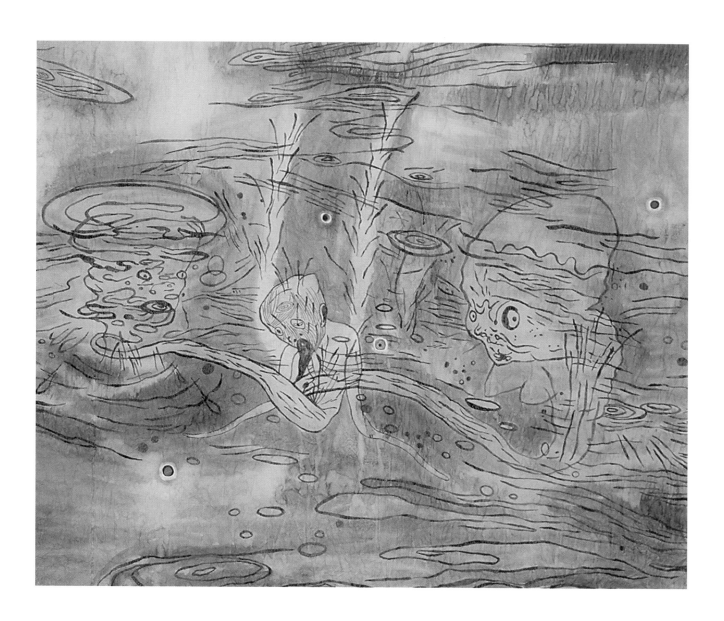

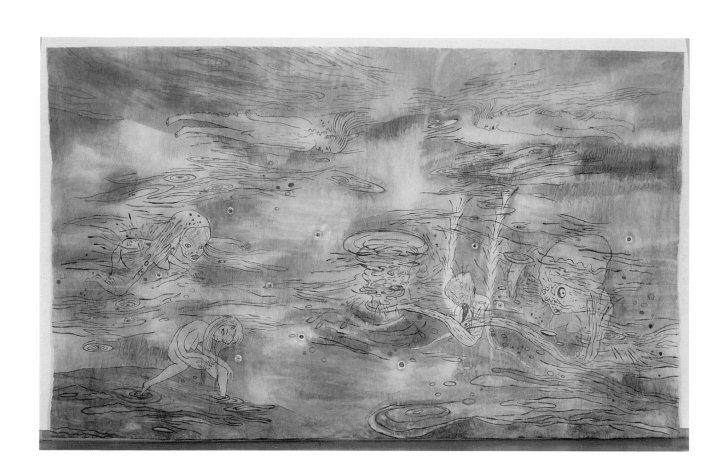

Water Gods Playing Tricks, 2003 (detail left)

Raphaëlle de Groot, *Third Person, Drawing session at the University of Western Ontario*, 2004 (performance still) Photo: Mirko Sabatini

A Brief Treatise on the Line[1]

[Louise Déry]

"A LINE IS A MAN," as Jean Genet so perceptively remarked of Giacometti.[2] However, the simplicity of this statement in no way negates the intense complexity that a few stray pencil strokes can produce basking in the paper's white light. Often growing out of an urge that is close to invention or investigation, these strokes are put together as an object of reflection coiled around knowledge. One may take a broad, decompartmentalized approach to drawing that steers clear of conformity to both its technical orthodoxy and its supposedly embryonic status meant to lead to a more "accomplished" statement. It then becomes immediately apparent that many artists practice it in the spirit of an intellectual exercise not *of* drawing but *through* drawing. Its analytical possibilities and relative fragility make it a space of conception and creation with its own laws, a space that strains and mistreats familiar geometries, and bends what is exacerbated in the so real and concrete world around us.

I have noticed that a number of artists like to lean back on the reading and writing that so closely and intimately accompany their relationship to drawing. Because of references to language, literature and even science, drawing has a nomenclature of manners and forms in which quotations, written annotations, diagrams, sketches, graphic states, building plans and so on find a way of lodging themselves on loose sheets and in sketchbooks. Whether the result of automatic writing or calligraphy, in its trajectory, the stroke is an agent of metamorphosis. It sometimes gives evidence of the development of projects that have remained an idea, hence an ideal, especially when it reveals that they cannot be carried out in practice. But still, it makes the pathways of thought and the gathering artistic act easier to follow.

Even when drawing resorts to other media and supports than pencil and paper, it is still concerned with all that flows from lines and strokes, everything that adopts a linear configuration. In many works, the use of essentially filiform materials such as wire, cable, hair, thread and metal mesh suggests the privileged status of stroke and line, and highlights an object's contour, skeleton, armature or framework. In this sense, as used by a number of artists, drawing — being closer to abstraction, language and concept — presents a formal and symbolic dimension that distinguishes it from other media. Between the formless and its form, between drawing's discretion and its revealed strength, lies the work of the mind.

Translated from French by Donald Pistoles

Notes

1. My title derives from Hubert Damisch's *Traité du trait* (Paris: Réunion des musées nationaux, 1995).

2. Quoted by Michel Surya in "Georges Bataille: une autre histoire de l'oeil," *Cahiers de l'Abbaye de Sainte-Croix* 69 (March-June 1991), p. 25 [trans. D.P.].

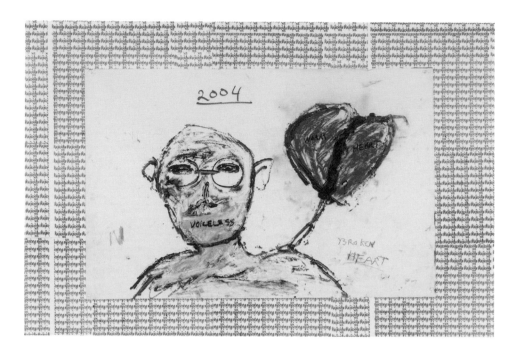

Substitute for the Prayer Wheel, 2004 (details left)

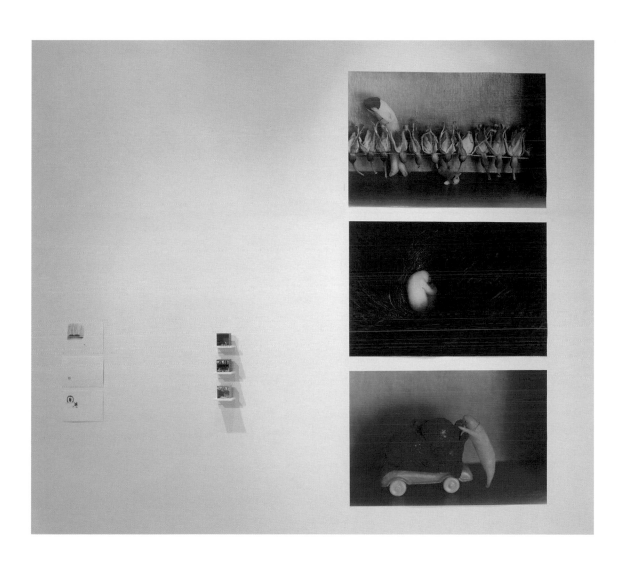

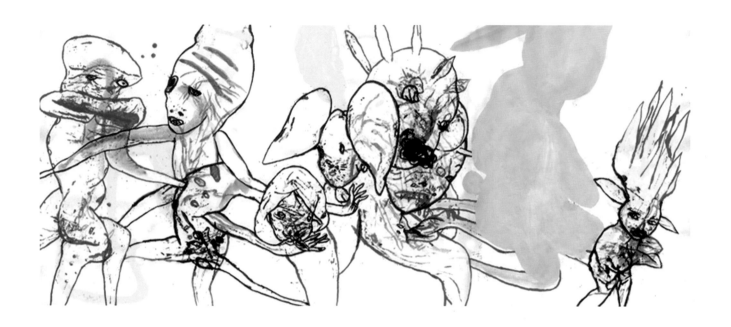

Ed Pien, *Glorious Pink Apparition,* 2003

A Little History for a Lot of Drawing:
A View from Halifax

[Susan Gibson Garvey]

THE TWO DECADES FROM 1970 TO 1990 encompass one of the most interesting periods in the development of Canadian drawing. It was a time when the definition of drawing was greatly expanded by artists with widely differing practices — abstract, realist, conceptual, process, minimal — and whose experiments in a variety of graphic media reinforced the idea that drawing can be as much an autonomous statement as a painting or sculpture. Prior to this period, with a few notable exceptions, Canadian drawing had followed fairly closely the conservative disciplines of the European academies, or the practical role of preparatory sketches for works in other media. After this period, until very recently, critical interest in drawing was eclipsed by a focus on sociopolitical issues and a sense that drawing as an independent practice had been absorbed into a post-Modern pastiche of media and techniques.

A striking example of the intense interest in drawing in the 1970s has been provided by writer Denis Lessard, who lists no fewer than forty-three juried or curated exhibitions of drawing held in public galleries in Canada during the decade 1972 to 1982.[1] From Ernest Lindner's meticulous realism to Betty Goodwin's gestures on mylar, from Tim Whiten's lemon stains and mysterious markings to Frank Nulf's sinister abstracts, and from David Rabinowitch's minimal mathematics to Don Wright's richly-worked mixed media surfaces (to name just a very few), Canadian galleries the 1970s and 1980s were filled with examples of artists exploring the limits of drawing media and processes. Canadian art journals also began to pay attention. Commentators discussed drawing's unique expressiveness, its role in visual discovery and the investigation of formal principles, in addition to its values of spontaneity and intimacy.

Why such a burgeoning interest in drawing at that time? In the first half of the twentieth century, the Modernist movement expanded the conventional roles of drawing to include the idea of the graphic mark as a thing of interest in its own right — the tension of a line, the expressiveness of a gesture, the texture and tonality of a passage of marks. In the 1930s in Europe, Paul Klee's exhortation to "take a line for a walk," as well as his Bauhaus colleagues' analyses of basic formal elements, encouraged artists to experiment with visual notation. In Canadian art institutions, the gradual acceptance of such formal teaching approaches helped to enlarge the range of drawing possibilities for mid-century Canadian artists. A number of American artists and teachers (many of whom moved to Canada in the early 1960s for political reasons) also contributed to these developments. Canadian artists themselves found greater support for their activities as the effects of the Canada Council's grant awards system began to be felt, and there was a general expansion of interest in arts and culture as the nation celebrated its centennial in 1967. All these factors opened up the options for Canadian artistic endeavour in general and for drawing in particular.

In the mid-1960s, however, all the traditional disciplines — painting, sculpture, drawing, printmaking — came under serious challenge. The forces of conceptualism, video, process and performance art, together with sociopolitical critique, opened up the possibilities for a radical rethinking of art's projects and purposes, and contributed to the rupture that we now recognize as the beginning of post-Modernism. While the rupture took place throughout the Western world, it was slow to come to Canada — with the remarkable exception of the Nova Scotia College of Art and Design (NSCAD) in Halifax where, in the late 1960s, traditional studio teaching was virtually abandoned in favour of "projects" classes and a (truly extraordinary) international Visiting Artists Program. Among the many "babies" thrown out with the bathwater at NSCAD at this time was instruction in drawing; it would not reappear in the curriculum until the mid-1970s — and then only in a minor capacity until the 1980s. One of the interesting results of this experiment was the graduation (not only from NSCAD but also from other art institutions in North America and Europe where teaching drawing was temporarily suppressed) of a number of artists whose drawing skills were not trained in a conventional sense. What they achieved despite, or as a result of, this situation is a fit subject for research (yet to be seriously undertaken), but it is interesting to speculate if their experience has contributed to the deliberately underplayed skills and "forlorn" or "grunge" aspects of more recent art practices.

The Dalhousie Drawing Exhibitions, initiated by the Dalhousie Art Gallery, Halifax, in 1976, opened a forum for critical debate at precisely the time when conventional drawing was under challenge. Over the next fifteen years, the gallery organized ten exhibitions, some of which toured nationally, and most of which received critical attention in prominent Canadian journals. An important aspect of these exhibitions was that the guest curators were all artists themselves, and their own works were often (though not always) included in the exhibition. The curators were selected from across the country and represented a wide range of practices, presenting a kind of mini-survey of contemporary preoccupations. The curators were, consecutively, Michael Snow, Irene Whittome, Greg Curnoe, Carol Fraser, Tim Whiten, David Bolduc, Robert Berlind, Sheila Butler, Claude Mongrain and myself. Our curatorial perspectives differed widely: assertions that drawing consisted of "unique works on paper" (the Museum of Modern Art's definition of drawing) were contested by proposals that any medium, process or technique — even sculpture, photography and video — may be described as drawing under certain circumstances; works that presented drawing as an intimate, contemplative activity were held in tension with large public expressions. The theoretical positions evident in the choices of the guest curators themselves ranged from formalism to conceptualism, from the textual and linguistic to revivals of Expressionism, and from the Modernist stance of Bolduc to the deconstructive choices of Mongrain.

Some of the guest curators went to considerable lengths to demonstrate the expanded field of drawing: Berlind, for example, included Paterson Ewen's incised plywood paintings and sculpture by Bill Tucker; Mongrain included photography and early digital work; and almost all of Bolduc's choices employed colour and paint. In fact, few felt it necessary to be bound by the logical expectation that because they were called drawing exhibitions only drawings would be found on display. What their curatorial choices indicated (consciously or unconsciously) was that the boundaries between the disciplines of visual art had become completely porous, and what mattered in defining a drawing was not the medium or method but the intention and interpretation — the manner in which the materials (and the viewers) were asked to behave, or, even more subtly, the manner in which the curator chose to construct his or her interpretation of the work. The cumulative effect was indeed to push the boundaries of habitual drawing definitions well beyond what had previously been accepted, eliciting from both audiences and critics acclamation and ire — and, as had been hoped, ongoing debate.

What caused the debate to falter, or, at least, to lose its urgency, was that political and cultural considerations simply moved the discourses into different territory, while the boundaries between drawing and other disciplines had temporarily become so blurred, and hybridity so prominent, that a disciplinary discussion seemed pointless. By the 1990s, drawing as a separate practice had dropped off the radar of many curators, while critical interest was largely focused elsewhere. Artists continued to draw, of course, and to exhibit their work, but few curators and critics chose to focus specifically and critically on drawing. Interestingly, from about the mid-1980s on, art-training institutions began to strengthen their studio offerings in drawing (life-drawing and even anatomy classes were reinstated in the curriculum at NSCAD, for example, as well as a more structured series of drawing courses). A re-appreciation of skills-based teaching has since occurred, and with it a revival of interest in meticulous representational drawing (but not, strange to say, much revival of interest in formal abstract concerns). At the same time, a completely opposite kind of drawing practice has developed, especially among younger artists, that underplays virtuosity and takes its inspiration from vernacular sources, popular culture, comics, graffiti and a fascination with the provisional, the abject and the dysfunctional.

The "popular culture" and "youth" aspects of more recent drawing activity formed the focus of the Museum of Modern Art's massive drawing survey, *Drawing Now*, in New York in 2003. Interestingly, with the exception of Bernice Rose's *Allegories of Modernism: Contemporary Drawing*, this was the first time MoMA had taken a serious look at drawing since they organized the original *Drawing Now* exhibition in 1975 (nearly thirty years ago). The current exhibition has received both praise and criticism for its "drawing as a noun" focus (or product versus process), a position which is discussed elsewhere in this publication. Most importantly, however, the exhibition caused enough of a stir to revive, at least momentarily, a critical interest in drawing. Current Canadian drawing could benefit from similar scrutiny.[2] *Just My Imagination*, with its cross-Canada perspective, could not be more timely.

Notes

1. See the bibliography in Denis Lessard's essay, "On Contemporary Canadian Drawing Exhibitions," in *Drawing: A Canadian Survey 1977-1982* (Montreal: Liane and Danny Taran Gallery, Saidye Bronfman Centre for the Arts, 1983).

2. The Vancouver Art Gallery has contributed a perspective from the West Coast with the 2003 exhibition *For the Record: Drawing Contemporary Life*, curated by Daina Augaitis. It focused on representational drawing by a core of Vancouver-based artists, as well as including several national and international artists.

above: *Untitled,* 2004
opposite: *Untitled,* 2004 (animation stills) Photos: David Tomas

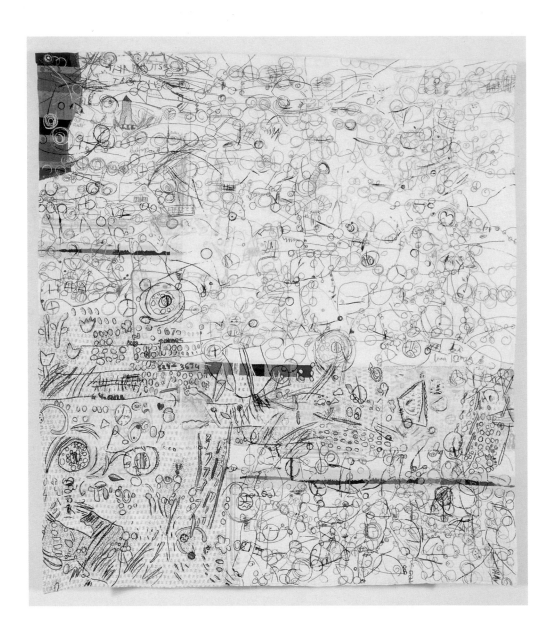

Draw me a car, 2004

Draw me a monster: Bestiary III, 2004

Works in the Exhibition

MUSEUM LONDON

Stephen Andrews
The Quick and the Dead, 2004
crayon on parchment
Collection of the artist

The Quick and the Dead, 2004
DVD, 90 secs
Collection of the artist

Sheila Butler
Study for Breathing in the Cold,
2003
charcoal and acrylic on paper
Collection of the artist

Essential Tremor, 2002
mixed media on fabric and
paper
Collection of the artist

Lucie Chan
Lingering and Leaving, 2004
charcoal and ink on paper, DVD
Collection of the artist

Remember? We Were Close? 2004
drawings, charcoal, collage on
paper
Collection of the artist

Michelle Gay
Swat (from the *Seuss Faces the
Abyss* suite), 2003
computer work
Collection of the artist

The Studio (from the *Seuss Faces
the Abyss* suite), 2003
interactive computer work
Collection of the artist

Cels from an Epic, 2004
digital print
Collection of the artist

Cels from an Epic, 2004
digital print
Collection of the artist

Cels from an Epic, 2004
digital print
Collection of the artist

Jason McLean
The Final Frontier, 2004
acrylic ink on paper
Collection of the artist

The Valley Beneath the Sun,
2004
acrylic ink on paper with audio
produced by Jeremy Schmidt of
Sinoia Caves
Collection of Julia and Gilles
Ouellette

Alison Norlen
Untitled, 2004
mixed media on paper
Collection of the artist

Ed Pien
Water Gods Playing Tricks, 2003
ink on glassine
Collection of Orthoconcept Qué.
Inc. Laval, Quebec

A Shamanic Ritual, 2003
ink and flashe on paper
Collection of the artist

Gathering for a Sabbath, 2003
ink and flashe on paper
Collection of the artist

Glorious Pink Apparition, 2003
ink and flashe on paper
Collection of John Latour

Fall of the Magician, 2003
ink and flashe on paper
Collection of the artist

The Puppet Player, 2004
ink and flashe on paper
Collection of the artist

**John Scott and Team
Apocalypse**
Substitute for the Prayer Wheel,
2004
mixed media on paper
Collection of the artist

Anna Torma
Draw me a rose, 2004
hand embroidery on linen with
silk threads
Collection of the artist

Draw me a monster: Bestiary III,
2004
hand embroidery on linen with
silk threads
Collection of the artist

Draw me a car, 2004
hand embroidery on linen with
silk threads
Collection of the artist

ARTLAB

Cathy Daley
rise/fall, 2004
pastel on vellum, 22 parts
Collection of the artist

legs, 2004
pastel on vellum, 3 parts
Collection of the artist

Raphaëlle de Groot
*Third Person, Drawing session at
the University of Western
Ontario,* 2004
41 drawings, four DVDs,
modeling stand, two display
tables, three bound books of
drawings
Collection of the artist

Luanne Martineau
Parasite, 2004
felt, silk organza, ink
Collection of the artist

Untitled, 2004
graphite on paper
Collection of Wesley Yuen and
Patrick Prinster

Candice Tarnowski
2003
10 drawings pencil, pen, pencil
crayon, ink, gouache,
watercolour on paper
Collection of the artist

2004
3 miniature dioramas, polymer
clay, acrylic, gouache, cardboard
box, found materials
Collection of the artist

2004
3 colour photographs
Collection of the artist

2004
3 drawings, pencil, pen, pencil
crayon, ink, gouache,
watercolour on paper
Collection of the artist

David Tomas
Untitled, 2004
7 lambda prints on aluminium
Collection of the artist

Untitled, 2001
CD ROM
Collection of the artist

Biographies

Stephen Andrews was born in 1956 in Sarnia, Ontario. His work has been exhibited across Canada and abroad and is represented in the collection of the National Gallery of Canada, as well as many private collections.

Sheila Butler is a visual artist, residing in Toronto, Ontario. From 1973 to 1989 she taught at the University of Manitoba and the University of Winnipeg, working at the University of Western Ontario until her retirement from teaching in 2004. Her recent exhibitions include *Girls and Guns*, work by a women's collective, Budapest, Hungary, 2004, which toured to Tirana, Albania and Novi Sad, Serbia. Work in progress includes the *Art and Cold Cash Collective*, an exhibition created by three southern Canadian artists and two Inuit artists, which will tour to Arctic communities and to southern Canada, 2004-06.

Lucie Chan lives and teaches in Halifax, Nova Scotia. She completed two residencies in 2004 at The Banff Centre and at Museum London in 2004. A solo exhibition of her work is scheduled at the Art Gallery of Nova Scotia in 2006.

Cathy Daley has exhibited across Canada and internationally. Her drawings are in numerous private, corporate, and public collections including the National Gallery of Canada and the Art Gallery of Ontario. Reviews of her work have been published in *Art in America*, *Border Crossings*, *Canadian Art* and many other publications. She is an associate professor at the Ontario College of Art and Design. Daley is represented by Robert Birch Gallery in Toronto and Newzones Gallery of Contemporary Art in Calgary.

Raphaëlle de Groot has a BA in visual art from the University of Quebec in Montreal and a MFA from Purchase College S.U.N.Y, New York. She is based in Montréal and has been exhibiting in Canada and abroad since 1996. Her recent exhibition projects include a solo exhibition at the Centre for Contemporary Art Le Quartier in Quimper, France (2004), and *We come in peace... History of the Americas* at the Musée d'art contemporain de Montréal (2003). From 2003 to 2004, in conjunction with the Pistoletto Foundation, she collaborated with workers of a textile factory in Biella, Italy, developing social exchange initiatives and a related exhibition.

Michelle Gay studied art and art history at University of Toronto and received a MFA from the Nova Scotia College of Art and Design. Her practice investigates the junctures between bodies and technologies, integrating a range of media including drawing, digital-building and computer programming to make interactive artworks. She collaborates with her sibling, Colin Gay (a particle physicist at Yale University), on software/hardware art projects. Interested in the possibilities of touch and poetics within new media works, they develop artworks designed to play with technologies in non-useful ways. In 2006 they will present a large-scale interactive 'stretchpoem' for Articule's series *Immersion*.

Luanne Martineau's work as an artist involves an imaginary play of historical and popular culture genres. She recieved a MFA (1995) from the University of British Columbia, graduated from the Alberta College of Art and Design (1993) and studied intermedia at NSCAD. Solo and group exhibtions of her work have been held at Trépanier Baer Gallery, Calgary (2005), Three Walls, Chicago, Illinois, (2004), The Contemporary Art Gallery, Vancouver (2003), The Fruitmarket Gallery, Edinburgh, Scotland (2002), and the Edmonton Art Gallery (2002). Martineau teaches critical theory and museum studies at the University of Victoria. She is represented by Trépanier Baer, Calgary.

Jason McLean was born in 1971. He attended H.B. Beal Art High School in London, Ontario and graduated from the Emily Carr Institute of Art and Design in Vancouver, B.C. in 1997. His practice includes drawing, sculpture, installation, sound performance, mail art and collaborative projects. He has contributed to several magazines as an illustrator, including *Adbusters*, *Made* magazine and *Bananafish*. McLean has exhibited extensively both nationally and internationally and is represented in Vancouver by Tracey Lawrence Gallery, in Los Angeles by Richard Heller Gallery, and on-line by Paul Butler's Other Gallery.

Alison Norlen grew up in Kenora, Ontario, moved to Winnipeg at seventeen and became a barber. Gradually attending classes at the University of Manitoba School she received a BFA, and went on to complete a MFA at Yale University. Returning to Winnipeg she taught at the University of Manitoba for ten years before moving to Saskatoon, where she continues her artistic practice and teaches at the University of Saskatchewan. Her work has been shown nationally and internationally and is in public and private collections in Canada and the United States.

Ed Pien has exhibited nationally and internationally at the Drawing Centre, New York; La Biennale de Montréal; W139, Amsterdam; The Contemporary Art Gallery, Vancouver; Middlesbrough Art Gallery, UK; The School of Esmeralda, Mexico City; and The Goethe Institute, Berlin among others. Pien is represented by the Robert Birch Gallery, Toronto and Pierre-François Ouellette Art Contemporain, Montréal.

Born in Windsor, Ontario in 1950, **John Scott** is best known for his *Trans-Am Apocalypse*, a black Pontiac Trans-Am with the Book of Revelations from the New Testament inscribed by hand into its surface. Scott's work has been widely presented in solo and group exhibitions across Canada, including the Art Gallery of Ontario, the Power Plant, and the Vancouver Art Gallery. His work is represented in numerous public collections including the National Gallery of Canada. In 2002 Scott was recipient of the first Governor General's Award for Visual Art in Canada. He is represented by Nicholas Metivier Gallery in Toronto.

Candice Tarnowski has exhibited and participated in residencies across Canada, the United States and the Netherlands. Her work was included in *Fibreworks: A Biennial of Contemporary Canadian Fibre Art*, *Puppets on Screen* (Glenbow Museum) and the *Alberta Biennial* (2000). She currently lives in Montréal where she is pursuing a MFA at Concordia University.

David Tomas is an artist and writer whose work explores the cultures and transcultures of imaging systems. He has exhibited in Canada, the United States and Europe and has held visiting research and fellowship positions at the California Institute of the Arts, Goldsmiths College, the University of London, and the National Gallery of Canada. Tomas teaches in the Ecole des arts visuels et médiatiques at the Université du Québec à Montréal.

Anna Torma was born in 1952 in Tarnaors, Hungary. She lives and works in Baie Verte, New Brunswick. Her exhibitions include *Through the Eye of the Needle*, Owens Art Gallery, Sackville, NB (2004), *Anna Torma: Embroideries*, Vigado Gallery, Budapest, Hungary (2002), and *Notes and Visions*, John Michael Kohler Art Center, Sheboygan, WI (1996). Her recent grants and fellowships include the UNESCO Aschberg Foundation's Bursary (2005); Canada Council Visual Arts Grant; Leighton Studios Residency at The Banff Centre (both 2004), and the Chalmers Fellowship (2002).

Biographies

Daina Augaitis has been chief curator/associate director at the Vancouver Art Gallery since 1996. Her curatorial projects have included solo exhibitions of Stan Douglas, Ann Hamilton, Brian Jungen (forthcoming), Nancy Spero, Gillian Wearing, Paul Wong, Zhu Jinshi, and group exhibitions including *For the Record: Drawing Contemporary Life* (2003). In the last two decades, she has worked with artists on new commissions, edited anthologies, organized thematic residencies for artists and curators, and curated spoken word, pirate radio and performance art projects.

Louise Déry lives in Montréal. She holds a PhD in art history and is the director of Galerie de l'Université du Québec à Montréal. She has been active in the field of contemporary art as professor in museology and art theory, and as a museum director, curator, and writer, most notably at the Musée du Québec and the Montréal Museum of Fine Arts.

Cliff Eyland is a Haligonian artist, academic, curator and writer who lives in Winnipeg. His paintings have been included in many solo and group exhibitions across Canada.

Susan Gibson Garvey is a curator, writer, teacher and artist who has lived and worked in Nova Scotia for the past 30 years. She is currently director/curator of the Dalhousie Art Gallery in Halifax. Her large-scale drawings are in public and private collections throughout the Atlantic region.

David Liss is director/curator of the Museum of Contemporary Canadian Art in Toronto. From 1995 to 2000 he was director/curator of the Gallery of the Saidye Bronfman Centre for the Arts in Montréal. His writings on art have been published in numerous exhibition catalogues and arts publications. Since 1994 he has curated and/or organized over 50 exhibitions in numerous venues across Canada and internationally. Liss is also a practicing and exhibiting artist. His favourite medium is drawing.

Robin Metcalfe is a writer, critic and curator based in Halifax. He works with a wide range of contemporary cultural practices, including visual art, architecture, craft and design, with a special interest in issues of Queer identity, gender and the body. After three years as curator of contemporary art at Museum London, he returned to Halifax in 2004 to become director/curator of the Saint Mary's University Art Gallery.

Kym Pruesse is a writer, artist, curator and educator. She is an associate professor at the Ontario College of Art and Design and has written extensively about art and culture. She is a founding member of the *off\site collective* and serves on the board of YYZ Artists' Outlet. Her curatorial and writing projects have included editing *Accidental Audience: Urban Interventions by Artists* and curating the exhibition *Urgent Witness/Drawn Remains*. Pruesse has been an active supporter of drawing through her writing and curatorial endeavours for over a decade.

Just My Imagination

CURATORS
Kim Moodie   David Merritt

EDITOR
Jim Drobnick

PHOTOGRAPHER
Kim Clarke
(unless otherwise noted)

ISBN 1-897215-00-2

Printed in Canada

© 2005 Museum London on behalf of the authors

Museum London and the MMB Collective gratefully acknowledge the financial assistance of the City of London, The Ontario Arts Council, The Canada Council for the Arts. The exhibition was supported by the University of Western Ontario and this publication through the Smallman Fund, Faculty of Arts and Humanities.

MMB COLLECTIVE

MUSEUM | LONDON

421 Ridout Street North, London, Ontario N6A 5H4 • 519.661.0333 • www.museumlondon.ca